3. Freedom of speech
for everyone or just for atheists?

All of this leads me to the most troubling contradiction of the New Atheism. The New Atheists argue strenuously for freedom of speech. They claim that religion represses freedom of speech, while science and rational enquiry welcome it. And yet Dawkins spends nearly a whole chapter of his book on the need to keep children from hearing religious ideas. He quotes approvingly from his friend Nicholas Humphrey: "We should no more allow parents to teach their children to believe, for example, in the literal truth of the Bible or that the planets rule their lives, than we should allow parents to knock their children's teeth out or lock them in a dungeon".[6]

Dawkins's answer to what he sees as indoctrination is his own brand of indoctrination: "How much do we regard children as being the property of their parents? ... It's one thing to say people should be free to believe whatever they like, but should they be free to impose their beliefs on their children? Is there something to be said for society stepping in?"[7]

It seems that Dawkins becomes the one who decides on right and wrong, and then ensures that the next generation are raised with the 'right' ideas. If, as Dawkins maintains, science and reason are so self-evidently true, why does he need to make sure that children hear only his world view? You can't help feeling that Dawkins creates a fundamentalism that's every bit as dangerous as the fundamentalism he opposes. Once again, his arguments are profoundly self-contradictory.

---

6. R Dawkins, *The God Delusion*, Black Swan edition, Random House, London, 2007, p. 367.
7. This comment was made in an interview with Gary Wolf, cited in an online edition of *Wired Magazine*: G Wolf, 'The Church of the Non-Believers', *Wired Magazine*, November 2006: http://www.wired.com/wired/archive/14.11/atheism.html?pg=2

me that Nietzsche and Hitler both argued completely rationally. If there is no God then there is no universal 'right' and 'wrong'—there is just each person's opinion. Hitler was completely logical in concluding that his morality was as valid as the next man's.

Dawkins's claim—that believing in an afterlife leads to evil, while believing that this life is all there is leads to good—simply cannot be maintained. For a man who constantly preaches that arguments must rely on evidence, we might wonder what he has done with the evidence in this case. Which brings me to my second point.

2. Atheism is morally superior *so there must be good and evil*

One of the main claims of the New Atheists is that atheism leads to a better morality than Christianity. They believe that good and evil really exist, and that they can show us why atheism is good and Christianity is evil. But their argument is built on a fundamental contradiction.

Take the following quote from Richard Dawkins: "In a universe of electrons and selfish genes, blind physical forces and genetic replication, some people are going to get hurt, other people are going to get lucky, and you won't find any rhyme or reason in it, nor any justice. The universe that we observe has precisely the properties we should expect if there is, at bottom, no design, no purpose, no evil, no good, nothing but pitiless indifference."[5] In other words, if you believe in his scientific, evolutionary world view, then everything is an accident and there is no such thing as 'good' or 'evil'.

You can see the problem: on the one hand, he wants to claim that atheism creates a morally better world. On the other hand, he wants to say there is no such thing as morality! It's a massive problem for his position. And it highlights a significant difference between atheism and Christianity.

I'm the first person to acknowledge that terrible things have been done in the name of Christianity. However, I can also show you that those things have been done in direct disobedience to the commands of Jesus. Atheism, on the other hand, has no foundation for even talking about evil. So when Dawkins claims that atheists like Stalin have done great evil, what is the basis of his accusation? Stalin was just following his own logical conclusions about the world. They may have been different to Dawkins's conclusions (and I for one am glad that Dawkins thinks differently), but if Dawkins is consistent then all he can say is that Stalin was different—not wrong.

The New Atheists want to have their cake and eat it too. They want to speak of a world that is accidental and amoral, while at the same time arguing that their world view makes for the most moral society. They are simply contradicting themselves.

---

5. R Dawkins, 'God's Utility Function', *Scientific American*, November 1985, p. 85.

ATHEISM IS ~~PROBABLY~~ definitely WRONG

There is a new breed of atheist in town, or at least that's the claim being made by the so-called 'New Atheists'. Richard Dawkins, Sam Harris and Christopher Hitchens have all released best-selling books in the last few years arguing that atheism is the only reasonable way to understand life on planet Earth. What's new about this argument?

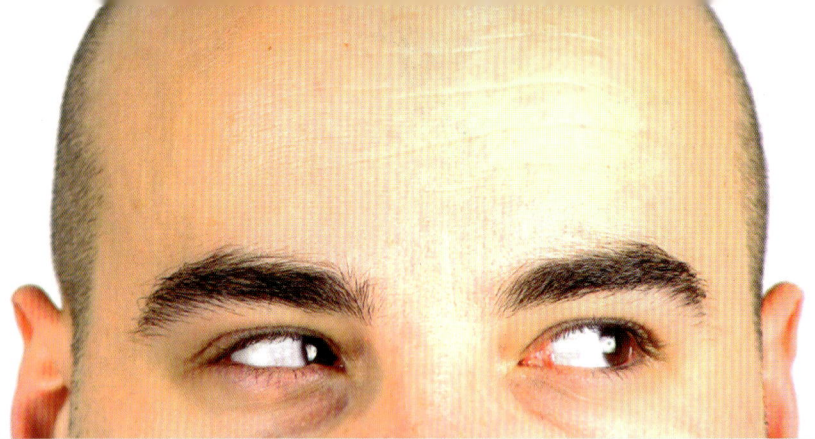

Clearly, it's not the idea that God doesn't exist— plenty of people have been down that track before. The 'newness' of the New Atheism is the argument that only a scientifically-grounded atheism can ensure the future of humanity.

Dawkins says, "It is fashionable to wax apocalyptic about the threat to humanity posed by the AIDS virus, 'mad cow' disease, and many others, but I think a case can be made that faith is one of the world's great evils, comparable to the smallpox virus but harder to eradicate".[1] For these New Atheists, religion in all its forms is the root cause of evil in the world. To create a peaceful future, we must rid ourselves of religion; and the only way to be rid of religion is to trust in science, reason and logic.

It is impossible to deal with everything these men have written in this short space. But for the sake of argument, let's take Dawkins's arguments and ask an important question: are his arguments and conclusions as rational and scientific as he claims?

Let me explain three essential problems in his thinking.

---

1. R Dawkins, 'Is Science a Religion?', *The Humanist*, vol. 57, Jan/Feb 1997, p. 26.

JESUS AND THE TRUTH

Jesus famously said, "You will know the truth, and the truth will set you free".[8] Jesus wasn't afraid of questions of truth, nor did he believe that force was required to make people believe the truth. Indeed, he was willing to die for the truth rather than force others to believe his views.

But truth is much more than facts about the world. Jesus taught that ultimate truth is about meaning and relationships and the purpose of life. We are not accidental clusters of atoms that randomly converge for 70 or 80 years of meaningless existence before dissolving back into the dust of this world. Rather, we are creatures of dignity and significance who were made in the image of God, and we are answerable to God for the way we have lived our lives. More importantly, it is only *because* God will hold us accountable that we can begin to make sense of life in this world.

Jesus said he came into the world because we human beings have made a mess of life. Deep down, we know that he is right. We have all done wrong; we have lied and cheated and treated others according to our own selfish desires. Jesus tells us that these things actually matter. They matter so much that he died on the cross because of them.

I don't expect you will suddenly believe all this just by reading a pamphlet. But I do hope you will begin to question the objectivity and rationality of people like Richard Dawkins. I also hope you will take some time to read the words of Jesus for yourself. He was the kindest, most moral and most rational man that history has ever known.

> If you want to know more about what Jesus taught, talk to the person who gave you this leaflet, read the Gospel of Luke in a modern translation of the Bible, or visit **www.twowaystolive.com** for an online summary of the message of Jesus.

8. John's Gospel, chapter 8, verse 32 (English Standard Version).

This was given to you by:

Written by Paul Grimmond
© Matthias Media 2009
www.matthiasmedia.com.au

ISBN 978-1-921441-44-8

1. Religion causes evil
but so does atheism

Why, according to the New Atheism, does religion cause evil? Dawkins says, "Religion teaches the dangerous nonsense that death is not the end. If death is final, a rational agent can be expected to value his life highly and be reluctant to risk it. This makes the world a safer place, just as a plane is safer if its hijacker wants to survive. At the other extreme, if a significant number of people ... are convinced ... that a martyr's death is equivalent to pressing the hyperspace button and zooming through a wormhole to another universe, it can make the world a very dangerous place."[2]

On face value, Dawkins's argument has a number of merits. Firstly, it acknowledges what we all feel: the horror and devastation of the 9/11 attacks on the World Trade Center. Secondly, it points out rightly that this particular attack involved the motivation of a reward in some kind of afterlife. But the question needs to be asked: does belief in an afterlife lead *inevitably* to evil? And is the reverse true—does belief in death as the end of life lead *inevitably* to good?

The evidence of history suggests otherwise. Christian history is full of examples of the afterlife providing the motivation to do great good at incredible personal cost. Historian and sociologist Rodney Stark contends that during the devastating plagues that afflicted the Roman Empire, Christians stayed to nurse the sick while pagans fled in fear.[3] It was a trust in God's provision of eternal life and desire to serve others that led the Christians to do great good.

On the flip side of the coin, the atheistic world view can be legitimately used to justify great evil. Godwin's law aside, Nazi Germany provides the perfect example.[4] Contrary to popular opinion, the philosophical foundations for Hitler's justification of the Jewish genocide came from the atheist Friedrich Nietzsche—the man who famously said, "God is dead". Nietzsche argued vehemently against the Christian morality of his day. He claimed that the source of true morality in a world without God is oneself. In particular, Nietzsche thought that the good in life consisted of wealth, strength, health and power. The way to pursue wealth and power was to create your own morality rather than just accepting the morality of others (which, in his day, was Judeo-Christian). From this philosophical standpoint, Hitler did not have to be irrational to argue for the Jewish genocide.

My main point is not that atheism leads automatically to Nazi Germany, but rather that the conclusion Hitler came to is one of many perfectly rational and logical conclusions to be drawn if the world we live in is all that there is. But if Dawkins is right, then rational argument must always lead to a better world. Unfortunately, it seems to

---

2. R Dawkins, 'Religion's Misguided Missiles', *The Guardian*, 15 September 2001.
3. R Stark, *The Rise of Christianity*, Princeton University Press, New Jersey, 1996.
4. Godwin's law states that the longer a blog discussion goes on, the more likely it is that someone will mention Nazi Germany.